Carusoism

216 Poems from Stone Sculptor, Richard Caruso.

By

Richard Caruso

ISBN: 978-1-4107-7824-6 (sc)
ISBN: 978-1-4107-7825-3 (e)

Library of Congress Control Number: 2003095508

This book is printed on acid free paper.

Cover Calligraphy by Richard Caruso

1stBooks – rev. 09/08/03

This book is dedicated to seekers of everywhere.
Whether successful or not.

PREFACE

At first glance these poems may seem to be just good rhyming poems. Dig a little deeper. May I suggest you study the poems <u>WELL ROUNDED, JOY NEEDS TRAGEDY,</u> and <u>HOLY SPIRIT TRIP POEM</u>.

In these poems an insight as to our purpose and answers to age old questions like why tragedies must occur? We may not always like the truth but I hope you find comfort in these realizations, as I have. And may I also declare that my experiences are so true that I would be willing to take the same credible polygraph exams that secret agents are required to take before being employed. So where some may declare that <u>CRADLE OF SOULS</u> is fiction. Nay, it is a very true remembrance, and it is accurate.

TABLE OF CONTENTS

THE SHELL

The shell of bell
At peace after rung
The free falling rain
As if undone from someone

From wax to wane
Whatever its name
I enjoy their pause
Till vibrating again

Vibrating from within
The shell begins again
Sending ripples of air
To ears which share

Share of the joy
Or which annoy
Of sleepy heads
Not out of bed

My garden seems happier
As the resonance swells
Spread like eagles on wing
Harmony from shell of bell

WHAT MORE OAR?

What more oar?
To pull for
Than quiet soul
And stomach full

As evening glaze
On ceiling lays
The oven cools
As peace rules

The oven creaks
Of caramel reeks
Oh so sweet
Makes me weak

Weak but not lean
The sun filters through
The back door screen
As my belly sings

THE CITRUS

Of heaven sense
What was sent
Of citrus flower
Oh sweet scent

The rose can not compare
With the sweet citrus flower air
And what fruit the rose chose?
Is under the emperors clothes

So pardon thee and give lee
To my choice of practicability
Bearing both fruit and sweet flower
Citrus is my plant of the hour

With no diet of rose
It only appeases the nose
While citrus also shows
Pleasure below the nose

TERRIBLE TO COVET

At the top
Of this pen
Sees my face
Put this in

How much peace
We could gain
By letting go
Of covets reign

I see it for
The thing it is
A cancer of soul
Needs a sieve

Bestowing so many problems
And it never gives
So much lost peace
Ensuring it strongly lives

Help push coveting away
Resist it on any day
Plenty of tragedies to spare
But coveting belongs nowhere

A great leap of mankind
If no coveting to find
Much fewer wars or fewer feuds within
All if coveting could sink not swim

BEFORE AND AFTER

One hundred years before the Beatles
The Civil War did its evil
Two great lines of history
One of joy and one of tragedy

Also of joy and tragedy
Just a year before the Beatles popularity
Was the gruesome murder of Kennedy
I was young but remember clearly

At first their pleasing songs
Seemed a little wrong
Just a year after the tears
With our nation still seared

But the joy was timed splendidly
After the tragedy of Kennedy
Made their songs all the joy they could be
And even more with ecstasy

AND MAYBE

I see all four Beatles
Strolling in a damp British field
With their backs to the damp air
Discussing songs they never shared

And as if loathing
With heads hung down
Almost whispering sounds
As their heels leave the ground

And of all the good boys
And of all the worlds toys
That they were still annoyed
Of not giving all their joy

And if by chance this occurred
They knew they had to reserve
That very special bird
Their spiritual nerve

NOT LONELY, NOT YOUNG

The more you know
The less lonely you become
The more you know
The more precious the sum

When we were all so young
And all so very dumb
We thought our mothers
Were the only one

She tied our shoes
And chased our blues
And filled our glass
Without having to ask

And in the store
We cried galore
If behind a door
As if she was no more

And it scared me so
Not to see her so
In a strangers place
Without a recognizable face

But now I know
What makes people go
I can read their glow
Without even telling me so

ESSENTIAL CHANGE

What others trade
In others made
Joy will fade
From constant play

Joy will sway
But constance dooms
Joy of fine
To simply do

Once a thrill
Now a pill
The constant will
Its own kill

Must make change
To feel again
A different joy
The spine enjoys

Like different poems
I now employ
At first joy
Later just coy

Long at rest
They might rebound
Though never again
When first found

THE HANDLE

The handle waits
For finger grates
From suddenly cold
To warmly bold

Never knowing
How the spigot flows
From the warm hand
That turns it so

But we can see
How the spigot flows
The handle only knows
The warmth we stow

Like some in society
Only a handle to be
Never thinking what they do
Further up the stream

ENCYCLOPEDIA

My golden home
And high school encyclopedia
Has given much more joy
Than the average media

Though I enjoyed the songs
Of the sixties phase
The encyclopedia taught
More pertinent ways

Though the television screen
Amused and informed
Education too little between
Amusement still the norm

Sometimes stacked upon my lap
While television babbles its fat
I cradle knowledge from A to Z
With books almost as old as me

FUN POEM

Shu ma lee
Shu ma da
Shu ma lee
Shu ma wa
Shu ma lee sha shu ma wa
Shu ma lee
Shu ma da

A quiet tear
A quiet fear
A quiet tear
A quiet street
A quiet tear of a quiet street
A quiet tear
A quiet fear

In the cold
In the heat
In the cold
In the street
In the cold of in the street
In the cold
In the heat

THE ROSE

The rose enclose
Which scent it throws
To bee or nose
Of this it stows

Whether apple red
Or white as snow
Its fame it throws
Like shedding clothes

Like petals aground
Without a sound
A bed to shed
Rain will softly tread

A dripping beauty form
Of rain or storm
Contrast with norm
Of prickly thorns

BOUNCING DAYS

I tie the ways of these bouncing days
Like string of pearls
While people swirl
While I may

Like leaves on tree
Which sway in breeze
But each sway differently
As if a life they lead

Past basic needs
Desire is the last feed
And the most difficult indeed
To seek or feed

But until these bouncing days
Bounce into some tragic phase
I further furl the ways
As if sugar coated glaze

THE WAIT

The wait is great
If all you make
Is on the wait
Becomes its own grate

Others are cooler by far
Because their options are
As numerous as the stars
Your ladder is of tar

Stuck on wait
The continuous grate
Like weighted slate
Its slant so great

It can be a tragedy
That waiting turns to agony
But thinking of coming pleasure
Is worthy of its measure

MY LIFE

My life is like a balloon
It easily rises or falls
With barely a touch at all
My moves are large not small

CARUSOISM

I was never fast enough for algebra
Or so I was told
So here I am with you
Exposing my soul

If an area where we lack
In others we bestow
Mine is stone sculpture
With enough confidence to hold

Like a stream running through many things
At its swiftest is where its clean
But the slowly rotating swirls
Are just cloudy murky merles

So what you do with ease
Is bound to please
What is murky and slow
Probably will not satisfy you so

Some are shamelessly supported by nepotism
I wonder where their scruples go
I study joy and tragedy
One could call it Carusoism

YOUR CHOICE

The poem of today
Is quickly on its way
As you read this
Easy to conceive this

You may be standing in a store
Looking for what only god knows for
Or maybe I underestimate you
And you know exactly what to do

The difference between this author
And some around me
Is I do not flee from the truth
While some seem to be on vermouth

I am not saying I am perfect
But my poetry tells more of a story
For good taste leans to the eclectic
But of their eccentricity I would worry

So if you are out to purchase a book
Take your time for second looks
Of which author gives more for the dollar
So a rainy day can be more pleasant by the hour

THE PILE MAN

The pile man drives his spike so deep
Makes restless bones of little sleep
The noise it pierces darkened air
While sleepy heads start to care

The work for bread and butter
Sent the night to quickly shutter
Another blow for another dollar
Another pole for another hole

Thoughts of sleep are quickly soured
As peace gets rarer by the hour
A golden tower for golden hours
A strangers work for sleep devoured

Eyes are weary of alarm clock hands
As hands surely rest on midnight stands
Thoughts of damnation surely abound
As the crew outside works the ground

Madness or fatigue will have to win
A decision to holler or try sleep again
To holler or…sleep…
To sleep…

NATURE PLAYS

I rest deep within this scene
Of waves that talk and beach serene
To every life dreams must cling
But here I love of natural things

The silver glitter of oceans glaze
Among the fish where otters play
The whistling winds that tickle waves
Bring shiny blinks to sunny days

The waves that meet the beaches edge
Seem to drive an emotional edge
Back to the womb with water all around
A feeling so soft and quiet of sound

A smell of moisture fills the air
With a breeze it comes to cool my hair
My feelings rise with every new wave
To every whim that nature plays

GOOD AGAIN

Deep within this lovely scene
I vision us and all it means
Our problems have past with glee
Our mood no longer too lean

LOVE YOU

Love needs love
As arms need arms
So hungry is love
A love open to arms
And so vulnerable a love
That is open to great harm
But open to happiness
That no other feeling
Can equally charm

YOU SHAPED

You have shaped my heart
Like wood on a lathe
And like the setting sun
You wet my appetite
With quiet waves

MORNING DEW

The sun kisses the morning dew
As soft as lips on dreams not through
A tender morning all colored of bronze
My soul is warmed along with the ground

With warmth the morning sweetens every sound
Like singing birds and crickets around
The innocent simplicity of earths awakening
Has risen my soul to this spiritual awakening

The sun I think is my moments friend
Without it all would surely end
And it warms the soul for you and I
And becomes a wondering candle for our lives

LADDER OF LIFE

Sometimes falling
From what I hope
To what I can
To what I note

The ladder of life cares not
You must feel your own ground
Before climbing above it
Your decisions ought to be sound

LONG SOUGHT GOALS

To make amends for long sought goals
Desperation can force a wishful role
The things we think we see
Like mermaids in the sea
Or gold under fresh turned leaves

Like wet fertile soil
Wrapped around a seed
A wish is only a wish
Until tears and sweat
Becomes its fertile need

TO THE BEST

You scooped me once from depression
Like a positive teacher giving lessons
And your beauty was like a spark
My life no longer all dark

Love all those who love the truth
And stay away from the rest
Let all lies lay where they rest
And move your love to the best

THE BROKERAGE

I thought I saw heaven
I thought I saw trends
I thought I saw growth
I thought I saw profit
I know I saw hell

I picked a few
And so did they
We both completely failed
But I was the only one
The one that had to pay

RARELY FELT

Your attention is like fresh air
And very real to me
Like the setting sun
Over oceans a glare
The days and nights
That we have given
Were given with
Such deep pleasure
That is rarely felt
From earthly living

MURDER BY RIGHT

After spoken confidence
And feeble tries
The kings and queens
Eventually hide
Behind the knights
And pawns to die
Hands have slid
From peace held high

The irony of honor
And gallant tries
Is murder disguised
Br righteous eyes
The right to war
Is firmly saddled
While homes and dreams
Are quickly rattled

THE EAGLE

Flying eyes
Above the trees
Soon the night
Covers what he sees

The eagle flies high
With talons squeezed
And cares not whose
Carcass he leaves

A POET

I want to be a poet
To write lines every day
And look in the morning mirror
To watch every hair turn grey

I want to be a poet
To observe the good
As well as the unkind
To prove I am not blind

I want to be a poet
Not because of any pay
But because I must say
What I feel every day

I want to be a poet
With words as a friend
To easily come across
While in your room or den

NEVER LET GO

If there is a place at night
Where peace is held tight
Never let go
Never let go

To make it alright
For someone tonight
Never let go
Never let go

We all surely know
What makes us glow
Never let go
Never let go

But if things come to an end
Remember when eyes would only send
Never let go
Never let go

CRYSTAL BALL

Many colors come my way
On every sunny day
My large cut crystal ball
With no moving parts at all

In front of a window it hangs
Streaming all colors it can
On the floor, ceiling, and walls
They continue down the hall

Reds, oranges, and yellows
Greens, purples, and blues
All different shades of hues
Brilliant beauty in view

You may take part of the display
The colors care not where they lay
Short, fat, thin, or tall
You are a rainbow from a crystal ball

ROTTEN ARCHES

Caskets are made
To wait for death
Who knows where?
Your final breath

A wooden bed
With ground as covers
So damp and sad
While it smothers

The casket reeks
With cracks and leaks
Time still not through
With the body you knew

The body will decay
But if it had a soul
It won't be for here
It will be to go

MY EAR IS OKAY

I have been saying what or why?
Not because it is over my head
But because before I die
I will know your weird head

Richard Caruso

TOO OFTEN

Too often it seems
We are like leaves in a stream
Bumping into everything
While others stay clean

To be stoned or twirled around
Like a sad laughed at clown
Or to move swiftly and freely
Where only success is found

This is what I see
Of the stream before me
But surely things may change
As time will rearrange

The twirling troubled leaves
May set themselves free
Or be displaced inadvertently
By a passing free leaf

Or maybe not so
Maybe some will never go
They will sink in their little sea
To have death only set them free

SLO

Maybe paradise
Cool summers
Mild winters

Green grass
Green trees
Clean air

See forever
Bishop Hill
Ocean breeze

Blue skies
Foggy mornings
Foggy nights

Central Coast
Cal Poly
San Luis Obispo

LIFE

Your thoughts
Your words
My ears

My thoughts
My words
Your ears

We speak
We listen
We think

We love
We fight
We dream

We change
We move
We remember

We retire
We sleep
We remember

We retire
we sleep
we sleep

We sleep
We sleep
We sleep

NOT RIGHT

The weekend
Was pleasing
Just right
Just right

The night
Is quiet
Just right
Just right

Bright moon
Is wooing
Just right
Just right

Hug me
My darling
Just right
Just right

Your headache
Is coming?
Not right
Not right

CAMERA YEARS

A moment turned endless
The pictures will freeze
At that very second
A thin slice of a reality

Just look at then
When life was when
And all as now
Important in somehow

We love the past
Like precious glass
Of what life meant
And what was spent

Spent with smiles
Spent with tears
The camera shuttered
Throughout the years

DO NOT STAY

What becomes of others
May be of importance to you
And on their thoughts of you
And what you should do

But honor their plans
You can not demand
Which only you agree
Or even understand

Your own happiness
Will need food
Arguments will destroy
The best of moods

If no more good times
Are returned in kind
Then leave them what they will
Before they send you a bill

DIFFERENT LOVE

Love is only love
To the beholding eye
Like snow from the sky
How much different now
Never one size

EXPECTATION

What is work to one man
Is almost play to another
So what is expected of him
Can not be of the other

CHRISTMAS CHILL

The pillowy snow
Takes us softly
To where we go

To snowy windows
Of inviting friends
Where Christmas just begins

UTAH

Winters snow
Mountains high
Valleys low

Golden deserts
Golden spike
Golden arches

Bear lake
Salt lake
Provo lake

Warm people
Cool nights
Warm days

Green Richfield
Cedar City
Ogden's view

Utah you
Always bold
Miss you

STEW YOU

Creepy places
Bloody faces
Halloween due

Spider webs
Pumpkin heads
Foggy dew

Moldy logs
Croaking frogs
Choking you

Witches brew
Torrid view
Boiling who?

Kitchen hell
Glands swell
Vomit stew

Screaming creatures
Midnight features
Ghost flew

Hear that?
I did
You too?

Rusty chains
Loud pains
Calling who?

Lost souls
Scaring who
Tread through

Deathly storms
Shocking worms
Maggots born

Fear unknown
Teeth worn
Frigid scorn

WORK IN HOPE

Dusty secluded corners
Dreary and depressing
Forgotten little worlds

Maybe once bright
Now just blight
Winning was thin

Considered only waste
Dark hopeless place
Horror of taste

What would change?
To slowly rearrange
This dying reign

Work in hope
Launch flower boats
Make fresh again

GIGOLO

It is not easy
To be a gigolo
You are at show parties
She made you go

And the ladies look on
From the corner of eyes
While asking close friends
Is that him, the guy?

It is not easy
To be a gigolo
The sly remarks
Take their toll

TO BRIDGETOWN

Take me to Bridgetown
Where to be quiet is fine
And old wooden steps
Have greyed with time

Take me to Bridgetown
Where I kissed my first girl
And people just talk
Of Bridgetown's own world

Take me to Bridgetown
Of maple syrup sublime
And the fall cool air
Of fragrant tall pines

Take me to Bridgetown
Where roads and dreams wind
And my upstairs bedroom youth
Holds a stranger this time

THE VISION

I dream of far away places
And of rainbows on people faces
With perfect days and perfect nights
Just one season of delight

I am not the first or the last
To look for pleasure that will last
But there must be a place for me
Where I feel comfortable and free

DAYS END

Winding down from any sound
Eyes are down with lips so round
Face is full with quiet soul
Body, feeling peace, so slow

Deeper, deeper, deeper
Drifting, drifting, drifting
Sleeping, sleeping, sleeping
Breathing, breathing, breathing

NUMBER ONE

To look after number one
Was never meant to be fun
Protect your life at all cost
Or be eaten by moths

No such thing as too safe
Pretty sures are high stakes
Do not play with mistakes
Guessing fools can relate

And if they had their way
They would laugh any day
Should you lose it away
By your assuming ways

To be too liberal
Will feed the Earth
While little sympathy
Becomes your pay dirt

FLOWERS UNDER LEAD

They try to tell me
Not to feel
Just do your job!
And be unreal

Am I the last one?
With feelings inside
Who cares about money
With a moral side

They force me to do
Rudeness to who
Question the task
Of the perfect staff

Authority should rule
But it goes to their head
And flattens all feelings
Like flowers under lead

I WONDER

I wonder
If I coughed up some blood
Would it be enough?

I wonder
If I laid on the highway
Would it be enough?

I wonder
If I melted from pain
Would it be enough?

I wonder
What it would take?
For her attention again

I wonder
When it will be
I forget her name

I wonder
If I will ever give
Love so freely again

ALWAYS SOMETHING

No such thing
As perfect freedom
There is always something
That needs completing

Richard Caruso

OUR WINE

A thousand rainbows
Race through my mind
Surge, surge, surge

The dam has broken
Impatient of time
Surge, surge, surge

The pressure is strong
Yet mellow as wine
Surge, surge, surge

With light kisses
To end this time
I lay in our wine

PLANET EARTH

The blue
The green
The sweet taste
Like sweet cream

The yellow light
The warm delight
Joyous with glare
Like golden air

The soothing wind
Daub the skin
To health within
As warmth begins

The scented air
Lush and fair
Refresh the mind
While feelings climb

WARRANTY FREE

I will throw it away
If it does not behave
The way I want it to
Makes my life blue

I just cut it away
Or give it to one
Who thinks it is useful
Or maybe even fun

But for me you must see
I love to be free
Free of repairs
And taking it everywhere

If refusing to work
While still fairly new
I toss it goodbye
And its company too

STATE OF THE WORLD

Many glued
To rumors
To news

Helplessly watching
While world
Half burning

The onslaught
The plunge
The devastation

Prayers abound
Hugging crosses
Hugging ground

Upward eyes
Searching peace
Quiet sounds

THE TRUTH

The truth does more
Than set you free
It makes you whole
And lets you see

The truth does show
For what they are
Not what they claim
They think they are

But the truth must be
Very clean and free
With no bias to hold
Despite what it shows

And like a mirror
The real truth reveals
The condition of souls
And all their holes

HAD A TOY

I once had a toy
It was such a joy
Under clouds or sun
It was such fun

Feeling better than some
I showed it to everyone
Like the next door girls
Who gave it a twirl

I proudly watched them play
As if theirs for the day
It was a sunny day
That quickly turned grey

As I picked up the pieces
And slowly walked home
How was I to know?
They were accident prone

YOUR FEED

A promise of feeling better
Much better than yesterday
Becomes a drug filled haze
An escape into a maze

And as the habit grows
So the confusion it sows
To match the very first high
A deluge for just a sigh

The vicious circle grows
The fun no longer glows
The piper must be paid
More problems everyday

No one else could delay you
Of where it all would lead
Now you scream for help
From squares you disagreed

THINK OF OTHERS

A lonely hill with pain
With no rest from rain
Like it was understood
For the moment it would

May your thoughts be peaceful
And of your Earth be kind
For somewhere while you blink
Someone will be crying

LOVE NOTE

As soft, as fur, as smooth
As sleek, as snow, as new
As round, as suave, as dew
As gentle, as true, as you
As fine, as twine, as two

REVEAL

Not quite smart enough
To see dreams come true
To follow most ideas
Till no longer new

But always good at seeing
Of people and their views
Or what the world can offer
And what the world can use

We all have specialties
Which come so easily
With just a little effort
Shows our talent to be

And so I write to show
What others fear to show
Or simply may not feel
From hearts as cold as steel

WHEN?

When the money?
When the woman?
When the dream?

When the money?
When the man?
When the dream?

When the birth?
When the death?
When the heaven?

INTO THE NIGHT

When feeling what we can
We open up the sky
And can not hide a thing
Even though we may try

You need not see through me
I have courage to reveal
All so deep inside me
My truth an open field

With open heart and arms
My heart has bruises from harm
From those who stole its warmth
By stomping on my song

But my song will never die
No matter how hard they try
A lover of what is right
I see deep into the night

SKYWARD STONE

With my long speedy arm
Launching skyward stones
Would any come to you?
Or roll through empty farms?

Is anyone beyond the hill?
Where my stones fall quickly still?
And do they rest in someone's room?
Or splash in a creek near a ducks bill?

A hill I could easily climb
I am afraid of what I might find
A hillbilly with a shotgun in mind
Or a thousand bees on my hind

So I climbed my mystery hill
To find what I hit or filled
There was nothing there at all
Just a duck without a bill

BEWARE

Beware of loneliness
It is like the moon
The more you look at it
The bigger it looms

Beware of what is not
Like unanswered dreams
Even if they come true
They become just things

Beware of fast riches
Where hope is the only steam
Where work is not involved
It usually stays a dream

Richard Caruso

IMAGINE

I dream and dream
And still not there
Wondered of the taste
As if I was there

I gather my dreams
For my favorite bed
And push them around
So deep in my head

Others count sheep
They have all they need
While I think of places
And desires to feed

To come to the point
Where the dream is real
Imagine how important!
Imagine how it would feel!

DIVORCEE

She whispered words like breezes
While staring silver moonbeams
And wrapped her love with lust
Because her dreams had rust

But somewhere deep inside
And always first to deny
Except when all alone
She sometimes cries alone

And if her pillow was wet
It had to be the morning rain
No freedom loving lady
Could be unhappy again

Denial has her by her own throat
It is all a sexy cloak
One day she may open her trust
To become more of the butterfly she lost

WHAT THEY WILL

Say what they will of me
Now or in the future
But they can never take away
My education of now
Or in the future somehow

Let them talk behind my back
Of how I stack up
While each and every thing I learn
Makes me more of a being
And of visions yet to be adorned

These visions yet to be imagined
They are the sparkles of the universe
As far and as awesome as the stars
Their secrets unfold through education
Revealing where important things are

THE SUSPICIOUS MISTAKE

I literally sweat and worry over my work
And the honest excellence that I strive for

Then along comes the hidden mistake
The mistake that is mistaken for sculpture

And it simply hinges on all of that
And may all of our mistakes not fool everyone

Less we all be fools
Then honest excellence hence spat

To keep me from getting too much attention
Beside the outside critics honorable mentions

The art league felt too much credit I received
And installed their coveting ways

Maybe even someone was paid
To put hinges on two huge paintings one day

Hinges qualified it for sculpture display?
It took first place for sculpture that day

To humiliate me with a loss in their painting way
They refused to recall their contempt they flayed

STREETLIGHTS

Like guardians of the night
I stare at the street lights
And listen to their humming sighs
As if to say tonight
Everything will be alright

Beaming proud with all their might
Positive light into the night
Tall and staunch in clearing the way
I wish they could steer
My life that way

WINTER NIGHT MOON TREE

Blacker than black
This naked tree
Full moon beaming
Behind this leafless tree

The dark and dreary
Has a beauty I know
That is only more eerie
With a full moons glow

With black winding branches
Piercing a cold starry sky
It almost seems alive
With moon beams that slide

Its deep black beauty
Mixed with a silent scene
Oh full moon of silver
Is its only quiver so clean

STONE SCULPTOR

The marble is wonderful
It takes firm attention to break it
It takes care to shape it
And way before I sign it
I have fallen in love with it

LIFE2

Life is like a banana
It is easy to compare the two
Even if you live an optimist
The similarities may surprise you

Start out very cute
As green as a weed
You are also short and stubby
A big banana you struggle to be

A lot less green
A little bit taller
Proud as a teen
Freckles by the hour

Today an adult banana
As big and healthy
As you will ever be
Fingers get away from me!

Your friends are all gone
The fingers took them away
You are losing your yellow glow
The freckles are turning into moles

You are sweeter than ever
But what was plenty of starch
You are now diabetic
Ripeness through its march

You are no longer firm
And neither is your skin
You are constantly cold
With your skin so thin

You lived out your friends
The last in the bowl
Here comes the fingers!
To save you from mold

But you were not eaten
You think you got death beaten
But the hand got your guts smashed
Then threw you in the trash

PAIN

The trauma is always there
To remind us of our share
That in a world of bread
We are suddenly under tread

THEREFORE

The dice falls as cold and hard as steel
Our fate falls as cold and hard as steel
The coldest winter winds are of steel
Therefore our will must be of steel

WACKY WORLD

I have never met a man
Who at one time or another
Did not ask to be hated
Especially by his brother

THE DRIVING JERK

One cold morning day
While deep in a sleep
My world was struck
Turned my car to a heap

I am no longer asleep
I am standing in the street
I can not believe my eyes
Who is this creep?

The whole drivers side
And the front fender too
Looked just as messy
As King Kong's doo doo

The wheel was destroyed
Along with its tire
Steam is now rising from my head
While holding eyes of fire

PARTY GOERS

We have finished our toast
And dried up our wine
You were ugly
Now you look so divine

With nothing new to say
It looks like a slow day
And contemplating my navel
I have lint for you today

With bellies all high
And IQ's all low
Our foreheads begin to slope
While the toilet makes ropes

We must look a disgrace
But we can leave with a cheer
And maybe steal another beer
Nice to make a mess of your place

IN SEARCH OF

What are you going to do?
When nothing seems new
What are your options now?
To get a life somehow

A sonneteer at best
Not close to troubadour
Not getting the brass ring
Out of your life it stings

Richard Caruso

HER ARRANGED LIFE

From the very beginning
You hung on their word
Words of your friends
And the war begins

Is it better now?
In your arranged life?
A life run by friends?
From which you depend

Would never listen to me
I was just to be diluted
In the shadow of your friends
Our love was doomed to end

I feel sorry for you
Not having a real life
Just chatty mindless tongues
Who stole my future wife

POOR MANS POEM

I got a car
That will not go far
With very little wallet fuel
Break downs are also not new

But when I love her
I do feel rich
I know of chemistry
This is more than an itch

My clothes are simple
And so is my life
Nothing pretentious
Could make her my wife

IT IS ALRIGHT

Out of failed dreams
Must a new hope arise?
A hope stronger than before?
Like a flower from ashes

Is it wishful thinking?
A trait of human kind?
A way of denying?
What failure had wrought?

It is not feeble
To think in such ways
The mere journey of struggle
Builds character every day

Yes and even more
A way of surviving
A promise of effort
A torch for the young

DECEMBER

With Decembers vision
Of what might become
I see much emotion
And total up the sum

Christmas is about our future
Christmas is about our past
And in between
We fill our glass

In hope of what
We want to see
That is what Christmas
Means to me

Richard Caruso

THE MARXIST DREAM

There is a superpower
Our government had said
That wants to bury us
While asleep in our beds

And to prove it even more
We saw Khrushchev sore
While banging his shoe
To make us unglue

But the winds of change
Along with poverty's reign
Changed many a heads
Communism was dead

The people revolted
The leaders had noted
From Gorby and Yeltsin
Try democracy instead

The Soviet Union
Will be no more
The paper said
Stalinism is really dead

VARMINT SONNET

I got a hanker
For the danker
A country bumpkin
With nothing to do

I love my women
Just like whiskey
And I am ignorant
Through and through

I got a hanker
For the danker
When I spit my chew
I lower my IQ

Richard Caruso

NOT SO BAD

I have a thought
For every blink of any eye
And I have sympathy
For anyone who cries

But I must advise you
Living day to day
If you are just getting by
You are doing okay

Give me a warm bed
A stomach well fed
I am losing my hair
But I do not care

If you are busy in life
And occasionally smile
Even time to dream?
Then glow every mile

Just enough money
To stay where you are
There is no vacation
Till you get a new car

Your life is not so bad
And romance you have had
Only the homeless
Are truly sad

I BELIEVE

I believe in more
More than I can say
There is a mystery
A mystery of the way

The way love comforts
The way a song can feel
A mystery of appeal
In every human thrill

WHAT IS WRONG?

And when the stars
Fail to make you feel
You are in trouble
Something must heal

The ripples of pain
Have put a strain
On all that you are missing
No doubt a shame

A waste of the heart
Get trouble off your chart
Until the stars are warm again
Your heart is forever thin

IT ALL GOES ON

When winds wonder through trees
The poems rustle the leaves
Almost religious to me
Like earthy harmony

The frost-the dew
What I once had
What I once knew
Held my life like glue

I change like the seasons
Just to arrive
You have been there too
I see it in your eyes

THE USUAL

Before you crush my heart
Let us pretend
It simply will not start

Before you say no more
Come to where we met
One more smile before the debt

Can we be friends?
Usually no
Everything must end

WE ARE SO FICKLE

When a good song is new
Like a good love is new
Every beat is good
Its clearly understood

As the song wears thin
Taking for granite sets in
Then down goes the love
When push comes to shove

Familiarity breeds contempt
With good feelings all spent
A newer song seduces us
Proving our fickleness

Richard Caruso

GUILTLESS CONFIRMATION

Like apathy my gloom promotes
Sewing those oats
My pleasure denotes
Time seemed to float

I scribe and I brand
My mind like sand
Sifting through gratification
Guiltless confirmation

HAPPY BY FAR

Not how hard you try
Not how hard you cry
Not how smart you are
But are you happy by far?

Not the expensive car
Not the beautiful spouse
Not the expensive house
But are you happy by far?

Not the many friends
Not the awards in your den
Not the boss who claims how great you are
But are you happy by far?

Richard Caruso

NORTHERN QUEEN

When the sailing ships stroke the stars
I am close to your heart
And with every Northern wind
I hear your name come in

Tonight the cold is gone
Replaced by a poets song
Your love melts the miles
As I dream of you awhile

And as the Northern Lights
Burn my feelings into the sky
I hope you see them too
As our love riding high

WHEN

When all love has finally gone
Then so goes the friendship
And when all friendship has gone
We were strangers all along

OUR HEARTS

Our hearts are as small flowers
We are moved by the smallest of things
What love has brightened and charmed
Any loud word begins to harm

HOW LOVE ROLLS

How love rolls the soul
The way lovers can sow
What we do to ourselves
For some pleasure to behold

Your love of silver wings
Has turned a rotten brown
Ears rung with heavy harm
Restless sleep will try to drown

Rise again to try again
And maybe cry again
At your own pace
Let all be erased

Richard Caruso

WET GREEN

So deeply green
So dark of bark
So freshly cleaned
From heavens stream

What woodlands consist of
Of the fog and mist of
Green sparkles of wetness
Sway leaves so sensuous

And as the breeze subsides
Oh serene therein lies
Darkness of the greenery
Heavens honey on wooded scenery

DEAR DYSFUNCTIONAL

I hear your reasons
Like screwy seasons
Life's unfair to you?
Life cares more than you

MAKING WAY

Fresh leaves of trees
Remind us of life indeed
To bear of Earths air
A newborn to share

To bud and unfold
Of natures planned goal
A miracle to behold
A new life from the old

No doubt of complexity
It is quite a reality
Here is beautiful growth
From ground to air we toast

From every star in heaven
To blades of green in woods serene
A promise comes near
From age of yester years

As growth has come and gone
Death starts to sing its song
A few moments of holding on
From others right to come in strong

RADIO SURFING

And in the middle of the night
When all are tired of sight
Our favorite radio we hold
As if part of our soul

With our nation in our hands
We also tune other distant sands
Hoping to hear other thoughts
Of what we ought to miss naught

Whether words to understand
Or songs in public demand
The human voice is a spell
From also the heart dwells

WHERE DO TEARS GO?

Peaceful and quiet clouds on high
Thoughts stay here as they roam by
Never sleeping and sometimes weeping
Before and past the days we die

Colorful portless ships of whim
How much history hides within?
Dust of cavemen or fields on dry
Of man and nature clouds rely

Sailing beauties of chance
A dreamers reality in a glance
Onward time passes by
While watching smoothness rub the sky

Large beauty grown by small beginnings
Uplifted spirits of where man has been
The air holds tears of men
Until the clouds rain again

TRY AND TRY

Like the falling leaves of Autumns trees
The glaze has gone from past eyes
With passion cooled and many goodbyes
There is still one thing I can not deny
My heart still wants to try and try

FLAME OF CHARM

Like the welcomed warmth of squeezing arms
The candle burns a flame of charm
Inside a circle of golden dust
We see a must of love with trust

For the moment your minutes are mine
Wrapped softly we are twined
Like a trellis under a vine
Your agreeable touch means divinity
As we face the night with serenity

AS WE GROW

As we grow our love with staring eyes
Not a single blink to make deny
The strength of trust from friendly eyes
A treasured companionship without lies

Richard Caruso

TO DREAM

A dream by itself
Is wishing at best
But to work toward a dream
Can bloom into anything
Even more beautiful instead

THE STARS

The stars are scattered angels eyes
A precious fantasy for lifted eyes
All thoughts of hate and dismay
Are lost in sparkles from the sky

If music soothes the savage breast
Then stars are dreams not yet reached
And teachers of wisdom without speech
Their silent highness draws our reach

Richard Caruso

EVERY FRINGE

On every fringe of every word
On every fringe of every nerve
And every fringe of every touching hand
There is my love to understand

We have come together this far
Not just to be who we are
But to glow like fire in a jar
Moonbeams filled with stars

THE ANTI CULTURE

Hidden whispers with dreary shadows
Of a dark and surly cast
Of this some love to bask

Prudence is foreign to these
Who burn wisdom like leaves
How they pry deviately

The hurting lies they leak
Like devil's snake they sneak
To make their pleasure quickly reap

A bellicose few make life hard to chew
Of arts and humanities they never knew
A life of scowl and midnight howls

As if born from spitballs
Like pigs from mud
They brush against clean walls

Richard Caruso

PART OF COLD

Tear drops wet the fingers
Sad regrets tend to linger
Of what comfort to bring home
Must be pampered by being alone

Someone's ego never forgot
Of a lovers bitterness
And of busted wishes
Never again begot

Like quiet Igloos
Oh so cold
Oh so empty
Oh so used

THE COMPUTER

Escapades of loveliness
They seem to escape me
While inhaling these plastic fumes
Tabled in front of me

Our digital world of
Many pleasures and fears
So many digits to steer
And yet so many tears

With all its power
It took my hour
My wallet it scoured
Like a bee to a flower

Hope computers are not television again
Where I wasted some childhood then
Where would I be now?
If I could refund that time again?

Richard Caruso

THE HALL

Have you ever walked an empty hall?
Time seems to stall
A barrier of comfort to all
Cold as the silence it calls

SUMMER DRIVE

Speeding to our destiny
Telephone polls come and go
Like some people we once knew
They knew little of us too

Where are we going?
I knew but say it again
Home again my friend
Where storms seem quick to end

To my right passes lives and property
To the front a road of direction
To the rear bridges long crossed
To the left my companion of seduction

As the wind fights our movement
And the road seems like one flat stone
You talk of kings and their thrones
But my heart grows eager for home

Yes dear I was listening
But my thoughts tend to roam
When thinking of life
I always feel at home

From the chrome the sun glistens
And the highway starts sizzling
The only thing missing
Is some unrequested kissing

Richard Caruso

RAISE SOME DUST

Raise a little dust
If it makes you be
What you should
Or deserve to be

But always be polite
And safely courteous
For other dreams spin
Just as sincerely with them

Your spirit or thoughts can dance
With agility that's self enhanced
By the good deeds or good wealth
Of fine happiness and good health

Kick the dirt until you are free
The goal may come quickly
Do not worry of the morning sun
Focus on your dream as one

DESERT GOLD

If the grass is greener
On the other side of the hill
Then it is buggier and muggier
So what is the thrill?

Some people have
So much time to kill
A mower in one hand
In the other Bug Kill

So excuse me
While you battle that lawn
I prefer the desert
Where I have time to wear my thong

While you are mowing
And pruning that lawn
I plan some cat fishing
Which girlfriend to bring along?

Richard Caruso

THE WINDOW

The windows edge of ice and snow
Brings us together
To make our Christmas glow
Our holiday we bestow

IT ALMOST SEEMS LIKE HOPE

And as the ivory serenades my soul
I am taken back
When I was more whole
Or at least I think so

Time has rusted my dreams
What was important to me
Was a beacon for me
Then pitch black comes suddenly

It serenades itself as hope
Around my neck as rope
Waits for when I think my ship is in
Then strangles my dreams again

WE ARE VAPOR

Like waves in an ocean
We are there
Then we are gone
Like ripples of air

And so we exist
Just moving along
To society's song
Avoiding all wrong

With little left
Of what we once did
The world could care less
Less worthy of a bid

This moment will pass
Like a cloudy day
Like a cold or flu
Unless it wins its way

For sickness comes and goes
But on its last visit
It refuses to go
Pray our savior shows

LIKE A SHIP ON A VAST SEA

I try to get close to my thoughts
Like a ship on a vast sea
In search of what I think I need
For stomach and soul to feed

And some people come in waves
Like a ship on a vast sea
Some beat the ship violently
While others meet me pleasantly

And so our just cause goes on
Like a ship on a vast sea
We struggle at times just to be
Our sails lead us to our destiny

MY ICEBERG EYES

A lovely old song
To make my iceberg eyes
With all senses on full
It vibrates my soul

I squeeze every note
As if a mate
And romance the song
As it warms my heart along

SIXTY FOUR

With a pounding of the drums
And the sprite plucking of guitars
Keeps a rhythm with my heart
1964 is nostalgic to some

All of that and more
In the year of sixty four
We were growing very fast
And aware of what society asked

To duck when we heard sirens
But be the first to the moon
And forever more be color blind
So forget what grandma said in June

Color television and music cassettes
Still fairly new in sixty four
Along with a British sound
That magic we all adored

We thought it was their accent
But the Byrds and Beau Brummels
Proved us all very wrong
So much with 'just a little'

So let the magic be
As elusive as it should be
I simply wish to declare
I too was happy to be there

DRIVEN

Like salmon running up stream
So goes the drive for me to sculpt

Sculptures of limestone and marble
Are innately beyond antiquity

The stone is like meat for my soul
A diet healthy and whole

And the calcium carbonate
Begs from within

We were once alive
Give us purpose again

SIMPLICITY

Simplicity is like sex
The more you try to enhance it
The worse it comes out

Because once you have enhanced it
It is no longer simple
It is a gimmick

Or worse yet
It becomes a chore
A tainted one at that

When it is raw and direct
With no guilt or permission needed
Then simplicity and sex are one

OH STENCH

Oh fetor of these fettered chains
That will not allow the moment
To rearrange
Hope of future time
To reclaim

STUPID

When you pick the nuts out
Instead of buying plain peanut butter
And you use a toothpick
A round toothpick to pick out the nuts
Anything dumber?

Richard Caruso

GOOD CHISEL

I am beginning to understand
The joy of a good chisel
The way it works in my hand
With control and guidance
Springing Art through its command

ANGELS

The slow piano is the soul of Angels
The slow violin is the tears of Angels
The white marble is the ethics of Angels
The white snow the bed of Angels

Every pure thought is a smile
Every straight tongue a blessing
Every truth is ongoing
Every deed of Trinity

Empowered by its own blessing
Not water or food
Empowered by pure truth
For pure truth be its blessing

Richard Caruso

MY FLAT CHESTED SLINKY

I love my flat chested slinky
And when she turns sixty
She can still move quite swiftly

I love my flat chested slinky
And when she turns sixty
She will get her occasional hickey

All you other guys
Fixated on big busted brides
There is something you must realize

You think you are in good
Till one year it is understood
They are dragging the wood

Your wife is only 44
She answers a knock on the door
Why she starts to cry?

Why it is my flat chested slinky
With her perky little chest
Almost as high as her eyes

While at 44
Your wife drags the floor
And regrets opening the door

I love my flat chested slinky
And when she turns sixty
She will need no surgery

I love my flat chested slinky
And when she turns sixty
Her nipples will be nifty

I love my flat chested slinky
And when she turns sixty
Again she will look under fifty

MYSTIC EVENING

As the night breeze romances my window
I am swept into memories
Like the too and fro of the curtains
The breeze is churning emotions

And the moon illuminates my window screen
As if it has a life of its own
Contrasting with green grass and shrubbery
It all has a mystic mood to tone

And as each breeze brings a tingle to my spine
I am swept back to innocent times
When naivety thought everything was fine
When there was much less clutter of the mind

As a child the stars gave comfort to me
As an adult their power and distance impresses me
As an artist they romance me
As a night breeze enhances me

Richard Caruso

ROTTING WAYS

Look at the buds
The buds on the tree
Come spring they weave
Into many leaves

Look at the leaves now
So young and shiny
Like fresh baby skin
We move through spring

Look how huge the leaves are
Just weeks ago they were babies
Now into full grown adults
Strong enough for a summer drought

Leaves are paler now
A chill wind reveals their thinness
But their size remains healthy
Death still winless

The leaves are haunched over now
And most of them a rotting brown
And those that were never healthy
Have already met the ground

Fall is relentless
A first deep freeze
Brings leaves to their knees
Deaths final fee

Leaves fall to make room for new
How similar it is for people
God must think we are not smarter
And maybe more feeble

When we are smart enough
To escape the rotting ways
I hope we also have the room
To not let our egos rule the day

FICKLE AGAIN

The children of Tropics
Dream about the snow
While the children of Arctic
Dream about the palm

For every yin
There must be a yang
Even the best of joyous love
Will soon miss something

One party is thirsty
While the other quite satisfied
We do not like to admit it
We change in the blink of any eye

THE WIND

The wind that parts the trees
Where does it go after that?
Or is it not as simple as that?

The wind that parts the trees
Is it refreshed?
Or simply there to rustle the leaves?

The wind that parts the trees
Is it more enhanced?
Or simply always blessed?

The wind that parts whatever
It must be more than just wind
Because it stirs my emotions
From deep within

HORMONES OF ROMANCE

The thought of romance is more
It is more romantic
More romantic than the actual
More than the actual motion itself
For once the motion stops
The thought of desire
Of desire or lust continues
Like music or art
The itch continues
The itch continues far beyond
Far beyond when the swelling
Beyond the swelling and the throbbing
So goes the hormones
So goes the hormones of romance

GREED

Be care of greed
Consume everything
And you consume yourself
Destroying your soul, indeed

TWITCH

To itch
Is a bitch
Especially in a ditch
Where the maggots twitch

FLEETING DREAMS

Dreams are as a plentiful as seeds
And like seeds only a few get to grow
Even fewer are fruitful
And even fewer yet
Do as their told

ODE TO CARRY

Drugs and alcohol
Are the devils tool
To be used on anyone
Willing to be his fool

Drugs and alcohol
More death than pleasure
And both are evil mothers
To dysfunctional measures

So Carry Nation
From heavens brow
Looks down on each
'You are on your own now'

And if Carry Nation
Could be with us now
She would not have to say
You wrought this cow

SWEET SAFFORD

I have seen the wet
The wet palms and redwoods
Of coastal Eureka

I have felt the fog
The foggy mornings
Of San Luis Obispo

But for dry winter heat
Arizona is hard to beat
Even Saffords sun is sweet

So if you are coming out of the Midwest
For the nearest heat by West
I say Safford will warm your chest

SUDDEN THUNDERSTORM

Like a thief around the bend
The thunder begins
No warning it sends
With no apology if offends

To take shelter is wise
As much as you try
For remaining outside long
Can do much wrong

The street drain runs full
Like a snotty bull
It is a gurgle show
Not caring who knows

And as the bad weather ends
Joy to us friends
For where joy begins
Misery wrought its own end

Richard Caruso

MESSY MIRROR

When I was a young man
I squeezed pimples too
Across the room they flew
Stuck to the mirror like glue

How the juices flowed easily
As if they begged to be burst
If they were any juicier
I would be taken away in a hearse

But now I am older
Not quite as much hair
And face pimples are rare
Barely any juice to share

Yes it is a small matter
That the mirror will not splatter
Bathroom history I can no longer shatter
At least I am not fatter

BATHROOM ESCALATION

I blew my nose
Onto my toes
But which should I clean first?
My toes or my nose?

If I bend to wipe the toes
It could roll off my nose
To only stain my clothes
Or drip on more toes

If I wipe the nose
Then what is on the toes
Will seep in between
Making the floor unclean

So I put my foot in the camode
While wiping my nose
Thought I had the answer
Until I looked closer
At my submerged toes

The toilet was never flushed
That ain't mud you know
So over to the sink
My toes does go

Richard Caruso

Balanced on one leg
While holding onto the wall
My hands were quite busy
I could not reach the faucet at all

So I grabbed a broomstick
From the nearby hall
To reach the hot faucet valve
Not trying to fall

But up high on the wall
Where my back was pressed
I noticed a large cockroach
Running in distress

He ran onto my shoulder
Then through my hairy chest
Like a slalom skier
Trying to do his best

I threw the roach off me
To only fall in the hall
Got quickly in the tub
To clean it all

AS KIND HEADS DOSE

As kind heads dose
The stars line up in rows
To tickle every roof
While the moon stares on aloof

Under the covers we roll
As the stars barely troll
You are not to think of them at all
As if it would spoil it for all

As hard to conceive of a scene
Just as sweet and serene
As peaceful heads of young and old
While the heavens unfold

Oh it seems they have magical healing
Scientist tell you they have no feeling
But on Earth something is reeling
That is not captured by logical dealing

Is it a blessing and that is why?
Or from some primitive drive?
I fear to analyze too long
For fear the feeling will be gone

Richard Caruso

TOUGH TO BE TRUE

Tough love is only tough in the short run
Because it starts with a solid foundation

Easy feel good love is only easy in the short run
Because it starts with a pathetic foundation

Satan likes the easy feel good love
Because you end up at his destination

Wise people already know this
But it is only the wiser that practice it
While the divine perfected it

SOUTHWEST

Bought some land
To take a stand
And will build upon
As quickly as I can

Midnight breezes
Cross the desert floor
Push my window drapes so gently
To make me hope for more

If you find a place like this
Then what are you waiting for?
Stake a claim as soon as you can
There is only so much desert floor

Once New Spain
Once Mexico
Of this Gadsden purchase
I do adore

At least 200 American men
Were killed at Mexico City's door
Never forget that price
They were willing to give you for

Richard Caruso

BANANAS IN BANDANNAS

Bananas in bandannas
Their skin is green when young

Bananas in bandannas
Do not pull on a cop he will shoot you for having a gun

Bananas in bandannas
They are bruised for life if you hit one

Bananas in bandannas
They are easy on your gums

Bananas in bandannas
They look like a penis to some

Bananas in bandannas
Do a circumcision before eating one

Bananas in bandannas
Many bruises when they are no longer young

UNBELIEVABLE

From back somewhat
My life my mother begot
To crawl before I trot
As my hands endlessly sought

Of all the future fraught
Coming hazards I knew not
Like a victim of Sir Lancelot
Of what cruel people could wrought

Whether their intentions good or evil
It matters not when under their needle
I am not saying as a tot I was feeble
But if so told it would seem so unbelievable

152

Richard Caruso
Richard Caruso

THE ROAD RAGE NUT

If you are a violent road rage nut
Quit blaming us for what your life is not
Minor transgressions can occur at any spot
Cutting you off should not lose control of what you ought

Cutting you off was probably not out of greed
But simply a misjudgment of your snappy speed
The person may still be wrong indeed
But it is no excuse for your violent feed

If you refuse to understand others needs
And you insist on being a bad seed
Thinking it is cool to be bad to the bone
One day we might send you to an Arctic island, all alone

Then you would be cool indeed
Freezing the finger off that you flashed to the public and me
Show it to the polar bear and see if he reacts nice
I hope he chews your head off to kick across the ice

FROM WATERS TOSSED

From waters tossed
Of what cost?
Blessed are the people
Under the steeple

From wings on high
As quiet as a sigh
Blessed are we
To take time to see

Of those of less
We feel from the chest
We watchers are blessed
For feeling no less

From bemoans of detest
Suffocating what is best
We pray you hate less
To let anger rest

THE REEL TO REEL

How I loved it
When the reel to reel
Spun its spell
Of the Beatles
And the Beau Brummels

Four tracks of stereo
On eight inch wheels
I was too young
To buy me one
But I stared at some

Near a store
Which held what I adored
At eye level display
Left and right cabinet speakers
Hinged like beautiful Mahogany doors

Like a brown Eagles beautiful spread
It got into my heart and head
A perfect mixture of wood and metal
And a weave of tweed
On the cabinet speakers indeed

The power switch gave me an itch
The play lever and recording gauges looked rich
Always loaded with tape and ready to go
Wanted to run it but feared my ignorance would show
A twelve year olds drool to make him look a fool

I yearned for the machine I knew I would never have
By the time in high school I knew it would be had
And this model no longer made
Or by the time I had a job for the money wave
I dreamed of being older and that machine I had

One day I got the nerve
To touch its beautifully hinged wooden speakers
They slowly folded like a smooth pouring beaker
Slowly hiding its eight inch reels and gauges
I cried inside of not having the wages

And once the left and right cabinets fully closed
They locked with a click to which I itched my nose
Licked my lips like heaven to behold
Stood back to stare as if it was mine
Like a fine wooden suitcase with a handle on top, I pined

LIFE IS LIKE OATMEAL

Life is like oatmeal
It does not always turn out right
But when it does
It is out of sight

As life loves us
We love it back
But we run from life
When dreams are sacked

When our wishes are stretched on a rack
It test our fortitude or lack
To what degree can we hack?
And return the wish to its right track

And always bobbing up and down
Our energy must be sound
A certain amount of good health
Is above and beyond even wealth

LEAVE THE CAKE

And if someone left the cake
Out in the rain
Do not be in pain
Though you say you will never have
That recipe again
It is not the end
You can still be
My dysfunctional friend

Richard Caruso

LEAVE THE ROSE ALONE

A rose may still be a rose
By any other name
But if you stare at it long enough
It will become defamed
Or worse yet go up in flames

SAY WHAT?

It's a lovely day
In the neighborhood
Hit you in your head
If I could
Would you be mine?
The cellar is fine

Richard Caruso

THE DAVENPORT

On her soft lap
I rest my continental woes
Like a befuddled map
My head ly upward in repose

My toes pointed skyward
Like Gremlins on a podium
They seem so far away
While in her torso my head lay

Her arms like branches
One on chest of bare
The other with cool leaves
Glide over forehead and through my hair

My eyes close
While in pose
They are relaxed in awe
Of the beauty they saw

Hair of flow and glow
Downward over each breast
A sudden rush of air
My own breath declares

CLOSENESS

Far off in distant view
Things and people seem slow
Only up close
Their speed and glow shows

The jet plane leaves its contrail
As if it bleeds
But if there
Its speed terrific indeed

And what of the moon?
What is slower yet?
Because they are far
It is every star

And if you get personal
The closer you get
No longer simple
Much more hectic

TO CLEAN

The fury of the duster
Scatters with fluster
Around the hucksters
Cleaning with muster

Too longer idol
Now scurry in hurry
To make clean as white owl
You are your own jury

And where is the line drawn
Where too dirty it becomes
Of its own brevity
A simple form of Einstein's relativity

THE TOP HUTCH

Reaching high to the hutch
Exposing her rear to clutch
Very seductively and a bit much
She encouraged me and my touch

Like a moth to a flame
I pretend to fall
And proceed to lean
Against the rear of her jeans

As my front torso did cling
To the rear of her jeans
Upward past the root of her breast
My hands careened

And reaching deep into the hutch
Our hands ignited in touch
Pausing for awhile
She turns her head to reveal a smile

Richard Caruso

AT MOUNTAIN BASE

On ancient snow
The mountain stow
Sifted white dust
Like angelic trust

The arcuate and arduous raise
To which the sun makes a glaze
With mountain ranges so parallel
Like a bilabial Earth it swell

And were it not
For riches sought
This view this road begot
As if it knew it ought

I collectively breathe it in
As if way past my lungs
And deep into my skin
I leave at last for the cold I shun

ALWAYS OF ME

Like the break of dawn
The ardent smile is long
The sun glides its head
Through a meadow like golden thread

But through my mind
My dream still tread
Of past loves bind
Of bodies entwined

And never of having sung her
Or having wronged her
But always of touch
Of me receiving so much

The haze and the daze
Slowly makes me raise
To shed my morning
Like a normal phase

A MANS VIEW

Shaped like a bilabial organ
Her firm puckered rear
I do not stare long for fear
Of her responding sneer

Like an upside down heart
The bilabial organ points skyward
To narrow to a tiny waist
While the lower half bulges with strength

It is that variance
Between large and small
That makes men's hormones
Climb the wall

It is like manna
For our probing ways
Keeps us from thinking
To keep us in a daze

THE LIGHTHOUSE

The lighted lighthouse all perched on lands edge
The lighted lighthouse all perched on waters edge
The lighted lighthouse between the wedge
All three as if Trinity

Its prominent solitary staunch
As if promise of firm substance launched
Obligingly anchored to the ground while ocean plays
It serves its purpose gladly as if on a tray

A beacon for anyone who fear
They know not where to steer
Or which direction to dare
Like a Holy Spirit always there

And when not used as help that might
Its glorious rise to heaven
Is ceaseless through day and night
It is all a strong symbol with nothing trite

THE QUARRY

As blasted stone
As if from foam
Flying high in air
The Earth beware

A sudden shock
Or ruptured rock
The quarries stock
To never mock

From life long ago
The quarry stows
Of bihavial shells
Of life once swelled

Of blast and drill
The dust does spill
To an airy soup
Into our living lungs it loops

I search the scattered ground
As manna for my sculpture point
At last a solid piece found
A promise of sculpture thus anoint

NOT ALL YOU THOUGHT

Par not all that you thought
Though all wishes scream
To succeed as a successful dream
Reality is often more lean

It is not settling
To be of head leveling
Mature is as mature does
Choosing the most promising of

The architects square
Measuring lines to be fair
Can not compare so fair
If you always change direction of their flair

And sometimes outside pressure
From life's unpredictable nature
Helps you to assure
Which wish wins the wager

Richard Caruso

THE CARS

In the seventies
I bought my first new car
The cheapest by far
The dealer said they are

A seventy three Gremlin
With a big straight six
And overly wide wheels
To get my kicks

Polished and dark green
It was a screaming machine
Hardly no back seats
Super light with front black bucket seats

The little hatchback could burn rubber
With its wide rear tires spinning under
Especially from a dead stop
Faster than a rabbits hop

Traffic is thicker now
Too dangerous for kicks
My sixty seven Fury
Is even more slick

Even though the traffic
Too crowded to flow
The Fury looks speedy
Just sitting as it glows

SWEATY GLASS

The glass does sweat
As beads of droplets
Sway from side to side
On a downward glide

The quiet adulation
Of all the condensation
As if rain it forms
Like a miniature storm

And as the droplets gather at last
At the bottom of the glass
A river or lake
The little storm does make

And if survived long enough
Whales and other stuff
Would roam its little seas
Unbeknownst to me

OH THE OLIO

An olio of things
To which these open shelves cling
And unlike the garage
These shelves hold a sentimental hodgepodge

The objects astrew
Like memory stew
More familiar than new
Of times past and what to do

Old movie tickets in the beak
Of a small plastic vulture
Polished quarry stones
Too small for sculpture

International coins
Lying submissively flat
Next to an old doorstop
That looks like a rat

And of the higher shelf above
A bamboo container as a telescope retainer
A hole in every finger of a sentimental glove
An old photo of a past love

ASTRONOMY DANCE

Jupiter, Saturn, Venus and Mars
Dance around us as if to spar
Since twelve they have caught my glance
While doing their astronomy dance

At a power of one hundred and sixteen
Their roundness beams so clean
Even the gap of Saturn's ring
That is what Galileo must have seen

He was born the same year Michelangelo died
Two great Italian men falling to only rise
Of this history can not deny
Marble and meteoric dust in our eye

The night is somber as it goes
In peaceful wide fields it stows
While jewelry above fly high
Without a cloud in the sky

Richard Caruso

THE VITELLINE BALL

A vitelline shade
Of morning haze
As dawn does raise
As dusk long slain

Of smell of wash
Like a pail so clean
Dipped from a perfect dream
Dawn caresses drapery seams

Of not to ought
From fraught to sought
The dawn of the window sill
The dream of the will

The waking conscious declares
Of another day to share
Of what the soul will
Within the body skill

THE FRISBEE

With a little wind
The Frisbee hovers
Then slides down again
At a slower spin

Left or right
Depends on the tilt you might
As it leaves your hand
To the other woman or man

With wrist of straight
Thrown on an upward grade
The Frisbee comes back again
Sort of like a friend

And you can throw it shoulder high
Or from the waist
Or lower yet
From the thigh

LOOMING LARGE

The moon looms large
As if the rear of a sow
Wondering far
From its trough

It begs for sympathy
For its predicament somehow
Its solitary show
As white as bluish snow

As full as a ball
It lights the ground
As if a humble mound
A weak white blue all around

And while the crickets
Chirp their crisp sound
The grass is bluer
Under a full moon bound

MY FUTURE HOME?

Winters are short here
Only at night it does freeze
And it is a comfortable cold
More mild than bitterly cold

I like this transition zone
Where my roots have swelled
Too cold for oranges
But sweet tangerines do well

Strung from two palm trees
My hammock beckons me
On my back and staring up
At the swaying palm leaves

They sway as I sway
From left to right
Like a slow loom
And I will be here till noon

Richard Caruso

HILL OF BEWILDERMENT

High up on a hill as if a dome
A person does bemoan
Of all the weariness
As if not having a home

Standing there all alone
Surveying the field below
With almost audible groans
Healthy yet inept as a stone

Absolutely no glee to see
Problems of not once
But twice and sometimes three
Lately relentlessly

Can not find a reason to be
So backs up to a sharply pointed stone
Falls back to stop the groan
And destroyed the gift God gave thee

And somewhere a woman
Bestows a burning filament
To replace what was taken away
On that hill of bewilderment

SLIDING FINGERS

Nowither the course
To the nth degree
Her attention is to me
Nuzzled comfortably

She is taking the lead
Of what she might need
Hoping it does not damage
My masculinity

With fingers like butter
Gliding from the chest
Down the front spine
Down to my vine

She seems to know
It does not bother me so
Her skin is glowing red
As if this couch were a bed

Richard Caruso

TRANSIT ENERGY

Like the arc to be bowed
Transit energy I behold
Transhaped into different molds
To form what the future might hold

Like the bargee of the oversee
Inventorying carefully
Taking responsibility not lightly
Yet open to what nature insist to be

The strife of life
Runs freely as if
The bark of a hardwood tree
Up and down its trunk inconsistently

Varying its quality
As to the weather
And the age of the tree
How similar we

MORE FOR THE GLOW

My poetry
Distracted me
Today's fat
Tomorrow will borrow

Was suppose to run today
But my poetry
Enclosed on me
While my track shoes lay

They must think
What went wrong?
The last time we played
We did okay

Little do they know
They are more than play
And more for the glow
My heart does show

THE DREARY BEAUTY

The swirly damp forest limbs
Twist throughout the damp air
Like tributaries end to end
With a scent they send

The bog as a spongy ground
Adds to the scent all around
While the sun seems not to exist
As if the fog wipes it from its list

As if a tripper from leaf to leaf
Leaves a mist from its wild kiss
The filmy air of fog is bliss
Before the sun becomes a hot disc

The dreary beauty looms
Dark yet rich of its gloom
Like one long soft deep tone
From a solitary bassoon

OH THE HISTORY

Walking the hollows
Of past lives
Including where my father lies
This graveyard can not deny

The summit heaves
All the effigies
And of the epitaphs
Like fading words of a phonograph

The tone is somber
As so it should be
The loudest noise
Of a whiny boy

Too young to understand
That these buried hands
Built this land
Upon which he stands

And though their souls departed
Not here but the place of their death
Their body still of Earth
In a place our weary hearts also rest

Richard Caruso

LIVE WITH YOUR CHOICE

You joke with your friends
About your ball and chain
And of single people
You call them strange

So of your own misery
Others must also sustain
You made the choice to commit
Little did she know she married a hypocrite

But just because I am free
Does not mean I have to take your baloney
Cross my path with an attitude
And I have the health to get you latitude

It is okay to be a proud family man
But do not call the independent woman and man
Any more hypocritical names you plan
Your obvious envy of our time is boringly bland

And quit teaching your children that singles are not straight
You hide that most singles are straighter than you by far
Not only sexually straight but emotionally straight we are
You over protect your children by never telling them the burden they are

THIS HOUSE

The lattice work
Contrast with murk
Of muddy puddles
Mixed with snow

The house is small
But throughout it all
The basement full
For a place of withdrawal

Owned by no one else
Unique to itself
Thoughts received from
Only this familysome

The hard day will come
When owned by someone
Foreign to its birth
Its once young mirth

THE SIXTIES WEATHERMAN

From the nineteen sixties
I miss the television weatherman
I miss his wooden pointer
And his squeaky black marker

Long circles around
Where pressure zones abound
Was when the marker would squeal
Like a mouse being peeled

When he pressed on the map
With his black marker as black as jack
The plastic map would rebound
Like a trampoline he found

If I remember so nifty
Satellite photos came in the sixties
Revealing real clouds of weather
Missing stick on clouds of tacky

When the satellite photos were strong
The pointer was already gone
Replaced by the zoom lens
And computer graphics
Before the sixties end

THE ROAD MAP

I drape a map
Across my lap
As if a friend
To no end

Of what it shows
Of places to go
To simply visit
Or settle in

The choices spin
And largely depend
On the mood I am in
To visit or retire in

I suppose it is endless
If for every day
My mind does sway
On where I might stray

Maybe to stray is the answer
Until I find a place fancier
Then where I have already been
So that my search will settle me in

Richard Caruso

HEARTY MEAL

Before I eat ice cream
I eat a tangerine
It leaves my palate so clean
For other things

I like my salami sliced thick
Half the taste is in chewing it
Not too thick or too thin
Two percent milk fits right in

And like the salami
I like my bread chewy
Stone ground and very firm
Keeps my body sturdy as a berm

With chewy salami and chewy bread
A little Oleo spread
Leaf lettuce makes it crisp for the jaw
And psyllium roughage to help speed it all

THE GREAT PLAINS

A thicket of thimbleberry
Outlines rows of corn in syzygy
And its pollen fills the air
Like a flailing mare

The zephyr blows top rows
To and fro they go
This warm West wind
Acting as bellows

With the Atlantic in the front yard
And the Rockies in the back yard
This the center of green and gold
Proclaiming feed for the world

And never forget the sweat
Our forefathers had to beget
To clear the bush and forestry
Feeds us no matter who we may be

ON STEADY GLIDE

On steady glide
The fog does slide
From bay to bay
Then onward to where it may

It wets the tall native grass
And around the trees
With equal ease
Leaving heavy dew on the leaves

Easy on the eyes
As it does its slide
Its life slowly dies
As the sun comes high

Where only the deepest shadow
It struggles to yet live on
But by noon
It no longer looms

THE DARKNESS AND ME

To quickly I am arraigned
The silent darkness nears me
It waits for my body
Like the dry ground starving for rain

The darkness comes closer
And closer till its eyes
Are all around me
Its loyalty apprehends me

It surrounds all
All that is in it
Yet nothing is ever
Ever moved by it

Light gives life
While darkness promises death
Like motionless seas
I was not aware of their powers
Until they asked things of me

I say no to darkness
But that seems to be of no help
While the family surrounds me
I feel the darkness ensue me

No! No! Do not let it be!
I wish this not to enter me!!
But my body gave way
To the darkness entering that day

All along the passing years
I knew I would eventually become
What I could never see
Now the darkness has become me

THE WAY I FEEL SOMETIMES

What is new?
Absolutely nothing
What is old?
Absolutely everything

If it makes sense
It is all very fine with me
If it does not make sense
Then that is alright too

Just as long as it does not hurt me
And if it simply does not appeal to me
All I have to do
Is simply raise my leg and pee

Because that is the way
The way I feel sometimes
Feel just like a puppy
Like a puppy dog under a tree

DYING TREE

Scream burning tree
Your soul is rising to the sky
Cry people cry
A part of your world is about to die

We pull the covers to keep warm
But we run from the heat
There is a person like this tree
Caught up in a repeat

For a dying dream can also scream
No matter how hard you try
At least a part of you will die
Shaking your head as to why?

SLOW DAY

Should I go to the park?
And expand my thoughts
Or go to my back yard?
And listen to the troubles
The troubles my neighbors have bought

WINTER PATH

Walking on a snowy trail
I stop to hear
What the creek and wind
Have for me near

The wind seems to follow me everywhere
But the creek plays a tune
A tune that sighs come back soon
Do not wait for June

Beneath my shoes
The crunching snow
The crackling muddy ice
Can not help but make you think twice

On this muddy trail
Of snow and ice
The dead brown leaves
A brown carpet for me

And like the finest felt
Green moss clings
To the bottom of things
Like large damp trees

KIND OF

Kind of like feeling too good
Kind of like cleaning your room just a little bit too clean
Kind of like doing just too much
For too many people for too many reasons

Kind of like doing
Just to be doing
And never knowing what you are doing
Because its doing you in

Kind of like staring at a star
Until you know it is far
Hypnotized by what they are
While someone steals your car

LIKE A SPARK

Worlds within worlds
It all depends on your heart
Stop, be silent, and listen
Can you hear it?
Can you hear the spark of your heart?

I know it says not on any chart
But my heart throbs after a spark
Like a sprinting Lark
Or a passionate remark

FIZZLELANDS EYES

A big smile arrives
When I see that nothing will fizzle
Nothing will fizzle in Fizzlelands eyes
Hard to deny

Pillows in the sky
Sometimes float by
With a smell of hot cherry pies
Hard to deny

Where flowers will die
If you do not stop to say hi
With a scent and a smile
That says stay awhile

Passionate trees
To sway in the breeze
Smart and lovely wise trees
That do not want to be
Brought down to their knees

MAYBE I WAS WRONG

If two can lead to three
Then one can lead to two
And zero can lead to one
Which means nothing can lead to something

And all of these years
I have been walking around
Saying you can not get something from nothing
So maybe I was wrong

And as sure as the rising sun
New thoughts may come
Complex are some
Weighing a ton

But with open eyes
These thoughts tantalize
To what I perceive as wise
Or what my ego in defense tries

THE HAIL

The hail does bounce
Upon the earth with a trounce
Like a white gumball machine
Losing everything

A sight somewhat frightening
The surge of white lightening
Illuminates the hail
Like eyeballs clanging into a pail

And the pitter patter on the roof
Sounds like animals on the roof
The wrong season for Santa's reindeer
Any bigger and they sound like a bear

As the storm is about to end
It switches back its trend
From hail to rain again
Eyeballs banging your end

THE OLD LADY

With a quiet demure
She sits all alone
On a park bench of stone
Thinking when times were

From a tree above
A leaf falls to her shoulder
As if to hold her
Glides slowly like a dream of

And she does not see the leaf
Until it falls past her knee
To the ground at peace
Like me soon she thinks, too easily

Here comes the bus
On which she depends
While some narrow minded children
Continue to offend

THE OLD MAN

At the corner he stands
Face wrinkled of deep tans
Like some foreign land
Somewhat gritty of sand

His hands as rough as stone
On one cane alone
His legs barely firm
Of the antique weight they bemoan

With a grunt he groans
To get going again
Inertia is his best friend
Tries not to stop again

And when he stops
He waves like a tall pole
Unsteadily as he knows
But his wisdom still grows

THE BLOIPING DRIP

The water faucet
Drips its drip so slow
Making this noise as it goes
Bloip, bloip, bloip

Each and every bead with a lead
Bombing my sleep as it goes
Into the full pan below
Bloip, bloip, bloip

I am so cozy under
The covers of my bed
But this resonance makes me red
Bloip, bloip, bloip

Its predictable rhythm
It continues to hold
Now irritating from head to toe
Bloip, bloip, bloip

Getting out of bed I would dread
While lethargic as lead
Something told me what to do
Between the night stand and your bed
Turn the main water valve instead

BAWDY WAYS

On slippery slopes
I denote
The bawdy ways
Of people these days

I would quickly tire
Of all their ire
Wallowing in mire
While walking a thin wire

So I opt for mellowness
Than rather the pretense
Of having so much fun
At someone's expense

And sometimes it is someone
Who does not deserve it
From their loud and lewd ways
Hurting fair people every day

BIRDS CHOOSE

What is it that you are after?
Some birds fly high
To go from North to South
To escape winters cold mouth

But while I am warm in my house
Some birds stick it out here
They gather on top of the chimney
Warming their tails from here

And every time the flame kicks in
The birds chirp with a grin
Like hearing a pleasant sigh
From tail to eye

So while some are willing to trek long
Others sit out the cold with some pain
Not a matter of who is right or wrong
The choice is equally defined as strong

So likewise in our lives
A definitive choice must arise
To chance the risk of long trips
Or bunker down long after the first nip

THE MARMALADE

The marmalade sings songs of color
Like a party in a glass jar
Or like a rainbow afar
Just condensed in a jar

The super sweet thickened fruit
Boiled from the opposite of dilute
The marmalade gels translucently
Sweet as a high pitched flute can be

And of what it use to be
There is now little identity
Only its color gives us a hint
Of strawberry, grape, peach, or mint

And once rid of its lid
I love the smell it gives
While deciding to use a knife or a spoon
I breathe in again of what it looms

ALL ALIKE

When I was a child
I would stare awhile
At the houses alike
Like one long dike

It bothered me so
Just to know
Of the future hold
To likely be another mold

Barely tall enough to see
With brother and me
In the back of parents car
We peered at the passing scenery

And still to this day
When I drive that way
I am concerned a lot
To become that mold not

And just as now as then
Despite their wealth and prim
I still view their position as grim
All so alike like one dike

THE PALM

Of all the plant life to see
The palm to me
Rings of the most harmony
Or because here too cold to be?

Crown and all
Like a moon rising ball
Like a circular water fall
The fronds reach high only to fall

Or like a circular water fountain
Its trunk as a center sculpture
Spraying out a mountain of fronds
Like an exploding fireworks bomb

And below its drooping fronds
Pointing straight to the ground
Like a hand massaging me
They slide as I stroll through casually

{Note, 'too cold to be' because I was still living in Illinois.}

SNOW

Of the glow
The snow does show
Firm as dough
Yet the cold it stow

Under a sunny phase
A top hard glaze
While the snow below
Remains like dough

Like ripples on seas
The glaze can be
Especially past three
When sun is on bender knee

Swallowing the ground
With no brown leaves
Except a few brown leaves
From a nearby oak tree

THE ORIGINAL TIME MACHINE

Many a years
Many a dreams
Of a time machine
Unlikely it seems

So say I
Watching who try
Struggle with why?
Not alone how

From print to radio
And video like television
They struggle with theories
And what they envision

All seem to miss a point
I wish now to express
Most simple of telescopes
May not take you there
But visually you are there

Your eye might as well be
In orbit around the moon
Just thirteen hundred miles high
At a power of one hundred and seventy five

And the higher the power
Of your telescope eye
The lower the orbit
Of your actual eye

It is a visual time machine
Visually taking you into the future
As if in a space machine
The telescope so simple and clean

And if you look through the other end
Like looking at the past of where you been
Everything much smaller now
If you had no lens to depend

Like the warping of space
To take you there
Bending light as if gravity
The lens does its share

WELL ROUNDED

Who purge their soul
Of lesser than whole
An unneeded olio
That had to go

On what allegory?
This ink must flow
To examine its lead
Its sturdiness is fed

Cleaning with thought
As is needed
The good is treated
As if weeded

But not to etiolate
With too much etiquette
Or the creative trait
Would meet its fate

For tragedy and joy
Equally annoy
They need what the other has done
Neither being anything without the other one

JOY NEEDS TRAGEDY

From the poem WELL ROUNDED
Have I convinced you yet?
That joy needs tragedy
Also study this seriously

From the moment of conception
In your mothers womb
The only speed you have known
Is Earth's constant zoom

But almost anything constant
Becomes numb to the spine
And that is why there is no sensation
Of Earths speed which is incredibly high

If we could brake Earths speed
Like a braking car
Then for the first time in our lives
We could feel where we really are

And things on your kitchen table
Would slide to fall on the floor
Just as on your dashboard
Your braking car puts them on the floor

So equally well
I say unto thee
Joy occasionally requires tragedy
So that joy may be all the joy it needs to be

THE WHITEHOUSE

The Whitehouse is to drip of blood
At first very slowly the inner walls
Then down the halls
Trinity calls

When the blood is outside
On the outside walls
At first our government will hide
Until the media ask why?

And all of the media
From around the world
Will come to Washington D.C.
To see the work of Trinity

And that about the same time
Both large and small
Both outdoors and indoors
All crucifixes are to drip of blood

And that many who had doubts
Will immediately understand what its all about
That God is reminding our leaders
The King of Kings is the leader

And that the blood will eventually fade
But not before photographed in every possible way
So that even more may believe
Our savior Jesus Christ gave us redemption one day

OF WHAT TO COME

The encore of the blue skies that boil
Of the climate to come
Which billow of grey
With constant lightning

When the lightning is done
A cross appears over the sun
Gold rays from the clouds take some
Silver rays take only the very young

The boil continues to roll
The rays continue to take souls
Until the night when the moon shows
Dripping of blood down low

Come morning the sun does not come
Everyone knows someone who is gone
Leaves are mostly gone from the trees
Some people with flashlights and candles in the streets

BUT FRET NOT

But fret not
The will of all wills
May put us through ugly spills
Eventually turning wine from swill

THE HOLY SPIRIT TRIP POEM

From one sleep
Does my body dare to rise again?
From one sleep
Will my eyes catch the light again?

And will the light be the same as again?
As the trauma of the miracle ends
How much longer does it spend?
Like ripples of history it sends

Is forever too long?
For an earthbound being like me
To properly conceive
As the way Trinity wants it to be?

Are we like pet fish in a bowl?
Going no further than the glass
Impossible to conceive what is outside
Unless a miracle does a task

I can only speculate
On how I will feel tomorrow
Do not get me wrong
This miracle has created more joy than sorrow

But like a mellow rainy day
Or the moment after we pray
Things are not as before
Opening different emotional doors

And like the yellow sun
It is fun for some
Or a torrid, miserable, heated day
Blinding the promise of what may

Always keep in sight
Of just what might
A miracle some night
To set things right

Richard Caruso

It is Trinities fight
To give us light
To cancel hated spite
So devil becomes trite

Gather your fears
Throw them away
Trinity always near
Made that way

God loves
Jesus loves
Angel loves
Special doves

Is it better not to know?
Refusing his name so
Only once in heaven
May I again see him glow so?

Silly is
As silly does
I still test what may
When I should be happy of

And so I am no more
Than Adam and Eve
Looking for more
Than what I need

Variety our credo
Seems built in
But to Trinity
Our oldest sin

And so heaven and me agree
The price to pay for variety
Is the added responsibility
One without the other flees

But to not tempt fate
Is the wiser responsibility
As Trinity warned Eve
Leave the apples on tree

Having never to toil
Yet wanting more variety
It would be one less fruit to eat
She also seduces Adam to more responsibility

With their first toil pain begins
A jolting reminder of their sin
Ignorance is bliss only at first
Forever quenching devil's thirst

But I have toiled
This advantage I hold
From devil's tempting variety
Holy Spirit knows I am bold

And choosing this wiser responsibility
Will forever set me righteously
In heaven I will gladly do as told
To trust my happiness for it to hold

For comfort, peace, and everlasting life
And a good distance from devil's strife
I will wisely choose joy over sin
The visiting Holy Spirit has encouraged my wisdom

Oh what wonders
Await for you and I
More beautiful than stars
In the darkest of skies

More elegant than the willows weep
More clean than a baby's first sleep
More comfortable than the best of sighs
More sincere hellos, by and by

Old man once told me
Jealousy is naturally
To want what others have
In that he saw no bad

Proving age does not always have wisdom
I usually stayed clear of him
Of popular people graced by bliss
They always angered him he hissed

The bigger the star the more anger from him
So what if they are threatened or murdered
He said so with a grin
Such a coveter I thought as I turned away from him

I want what you have he said
And you want what I have he also said
I almost brought up the Bible to him
But opted to keep peace at the job I was in

There are too many like him
And too few like me
Keeping goals of purity
While coveters bed with devil's scrutiny

So why waste time with a fool
Who thinks it is natural to be cruel
His hissing coveting ways
Is bound to upset heaven some day

A popular song came to be
In the twentieth century
You are nobody till somebody loves you
Now I know why that line always bothered me

It is not true to Trinity
Of Earth you need nobody
Can not you see?
Everlasting love of Trinity is purity

So fret not of who comes or goes
Your focus must run long
To appease Trinity as you go
To please Jesus you are never wrong

If science could give you a thousand years
There would still be accidents to fear
Then where would you be?
Under a semi you still need Trinity

So waste no time to declare
Of what heaven offers to share
Do not let coveters declare
There is nothing more beyond our air

Should the bamboo grow skywardly
Is it still a grass or now a tree?
Just keep your focus on Trinity
And let things be what they will be

To all you naysayers
Who have cursed Trinity
Claiming that in this dimension
Way too many cold tragedies

In the coldest of colds
Even science agrees
There still remains a glimmer of heat
A testimony to the other dimensions purity

And of this constant happiness
You claim you wish to always be
By what good comparable measure?
For heat needs cold for its own identity

For clear skies need gloomy skies
To be appreciated verily
A small tree needs a BIG TREE
To be called cute indeed

So equally well
I say unto thee
Joy occasionally requires tragedy
So that joy may be all the joy it needs to be

This along with this reality
Trinity has long range goals equaling eternity
It is a goal beyond our mortal possibility
And occasional sorrow may go with the territory

As this poem nears its end
I hope it becomes your friend
And that all coveters everywhere
Should turn their thoughts to just take care

For in heaven coveting will not be allowed
So on Earth each coveter should pray
To be given more light today
Or risk in hell to be disemboweled

For it pleases all
That all that always was
The king of all kings
As pure as white doves

Do not weaken to give in
To devil's tempting sin
Ask for the Lords anointing
He works often from within

And should a miracle come your way
Never let his message slip away
He came to help me one night
"Never forget that a miracle occurred tonight"

PRELUDE TO CRADLE OF SOULS

Things of three
Bleed through me
Things on high
Wet my eye

Always protecting me
Any evil knows
My anointed glow
Is forever stowed

Day by day
Week by week
Month by month
Waves of three's

Not at once
But gradually
Pushing with care
I am aware

Never with words
But as clear
Push on me
Beyond my ear

Your will is my duty
But always with care
In that we share
No need for flair

If ever a flow
On which I bestow
I lay my duty
On quiet clouds

If were my ears
Not there at all
No less the clear
Trinity shouting its all

CRADLE OF SOULS

I see
Yet I have no eyes
I hear communication
Yet I have no ears

I understand
Yet I know no language
They tell me I am as they are
A floating bluish grey sphere

We have energy
Yet we need no food or water
We have personalities
Yet we have no faces

We have a glow
Yet some more than others
We can not leave
Yet we continue to hold

We have no hearts or lungs
Yet we are told
We do have a purpose
Only not yet told

We have no brains
Yet we understand
Some spheres are open to friendship
While others don't commune at all

The centuries go on
I continue to hold
My friend tells me he/she must go
I cry but I have no tears

No possible tears to comfort my cry
I pleaded, "No-no-no."
You are my best friend
How can you betray me?

They are forcing me, he/she said
They didn't tell me, I pleaded
Where are you going?
I'm not sure, he/she said

When it is your time to go
You too will have to go
Then I hope you will remember me
Above all of this I too will miss you

Many years went by
Still waiting my turn
In a floating scene of spheres
I was of less joy

For one reason
My best spheres were gone
And the promise of future purpose
Was wearing thin on me

But there was still the overseer
She tended us quite tirelessly
In a white flowing robe
She glided with no feet that I could see

And in Trinities non verbal way
She occasionally kept company with me
Why so stressed?, she nurtured to me
No purpose to fill, was often my plea

At times a man would glide to the overseer
They would exchange lines
Then one day without warning
He raised his right arm and pointed to me

This one is more sensitive than the others
He will suffer much pain
And the overseer replied
But by the same way

He will enjoy joy
More than the others
And the man nodded in agreement
And for awhile he continued his stay

At times I could hear elsewhere
The going ons in heaven
Then from afar
Long golden horns did blow

And while the horns did blow
I saw the ugliest of beast riding equally ugly beast
They rode from left to right
We the cradle of souls were full of fright

And I must have trembled the most
There were no walls and the beast were too close
The overseer did her duty well
Hugging me proudly in front of it all

After that event
Envy seeped into the cradle of souls
I had already lost my best spheres
They thought the overseer showed favor

And some spheres I could no longer trust
And some as always
Continued no commune at all
I more alone than ever

Many years continue to go by
And after seeing the ugliest of beast
I pleaded that I wished forever to stay
Forever safe from evil ways

But the overseer did say
All of you must go
You were made here for a purpose to go
And I quickly replied

If that is the only way
Then when will I go?
And she quickly replied
I do not know

Many years went by
And without any warning
The overseer leaned over me
And said it was time to go

And the sphere of most rapport
Replied in this fashion
"No, no, no, I don't want him to go."
But I must go I replied

And before I could say
Farewell to the cradle of souls
I was in my mothers womb
My earthly overseer

All was dark
Loud thumpings and rushing of blood
It all frightened me
I communicated with heavens overseer

Overseer what is happening to me?
And this she quickly replied
You are with your earthly mother now
And I quickly replied

Is this the way it is forever to be?
No you will be born soon
Then everything will change
And then I replied

Will it take as long as in your cradle?
No, barely in the twinkling of an eye
What's an eye?
I replied

You will be fine
Was the last line from the overseer
And what seemed like 5 minutes later
I was physically born into earths world

It is late in the year of 1951
While leaning over my earthly cradle
My parents give warm smiles
I awkwardly flail these strange appendages called arms

And I am sad to soon learn
That the non verbal communication
Inherited from the cradle of souls
Was not getting through to either parent

And so like the lot of you
I eventually surrendered to language
Flapping my tongue between grunts
It still seems second rate to the first cradle

With all credit due
No figure of speech involved
The bible repeatedly claims
We are children of God

And this I would have never dreamed
Our sweet bluish grey and tainted off white centered souls
First born in heaven not earth
Blessed are the cradle of souls

Knowing now that we were always of first of heaven
Waiting while gently bobbing up and down for many years
Waiting for earthly mothers and fathers to be chosen for us
Knowing all of this how can we continue to harm others as we do?

This currently concludes the book of CARUSOISM.

ABOUT THE AUTHOR

Richard Caruso was born, raised, and lived most of his life in Peoria, Illinois until October, 2001, where upon he moved to Safford, Arizona, for the shorter winters.